THE

SCOTTISH

HIGHLANDS

Descriptive text by Robert Kemp

A Jarrold 'Sandringham' book published by Jarrold Colour Publications / Norwich

1

'Ye Highlands and ye Lowlands' says the ancient ballad, and all Scotland is encompassed in that address, even although the Islands may complain that they have been left out. The very words 'the Highlands' conjure up a vision of that grand and beautiful region lying north and west of the Grampians, the great diagonal range which once halted the legions of Rome. In our mind's eye we see the soaring peaks, the shimmering lochs, the secluded glens, the brooding green of the pines, the prodigal gold of the bracken in autumn. We catch the fragrance of the heather and hear again the call of curlews and grouse. And we think of history, of clans, of tartan, of feuds, of the claymore. True Highland scenery begins on the threshold of Glasgow, for example near Ardlui at the northern end of Loch Lomond **1**. The hills are in Argyll, and in Argyll, too, Loch Awe, with Kilchurn Castle **2**. The peaks of Ben Cruachan ('Cruachan' is the slogan of Clan Campbell) tower above this noble ruin.

3

Argyll also boasts of one of the most charming towns in all Scotland, Oban **3**, situated on its sheltered bay with views towards the bens of Mull and of Morvern. It makes a delightful centre of exploration of the beauties of this district of surpassing loveliness, such as Glen Etive **4** or, further to the west, Glen Orchy **5**, down which the River Orchy tumbles to lose itself in Loch Awe. To the high country a little to the west, as at Tyndrum with its guardian Beinn Odhar **6**, the first touch of winter brings a stirring transformation, never seen by the summer visitor.

4

7

8

10

Perthshire has many stretches of river scenery, such as that we enjoy of the River Dochart from the old bridge at Killin **7**, and Argyll, which has shown us the felicity of its sea lochs, can show a sterner face, as at Lochan Nah-Achlaise **8**, communing with the solitude of the Black Mount, or, at the gate to Glencoe where Black Rock Cottage is dwarfed by Buachaille Etive Mor **9**. Then, approaching Loch Leven, we come upon the grim Three Sisters of Glencoe **10** flanking the glen of present beauty and tragic memory.

11

Having won the northern shore of Loch Leven, either by the car ferry at Ballachulish or by travelling round the head of the loch at Kinlochleven, we pause to look back across the water at the Pap of Glencoe **11**, which guards the northern approach to Glencoe. Another fine view across the water is towards Ben Vair **12**, here seen with a cap of snow. It was on a bitter winter's day in 1692, with snow on the ground, that the Macdonalds of Glencoe were massacred in circumstances of peculiar treachery. Much of the land is now the property of the National Trust for Scotland; there is a fine modern road through the glen, which is visited by skiers in winter, but the happier associations of holidaytime never quite obliterate the old historical scar. Leaving Loch Leven behind we pass along the eastern shore of the upper reach of Loch Linnhe towards Fort William. Looking across the loch we enjoy an entrancing view of Ardgour and the wild country that stretches towards Ardnamurchan and the western ocean.

13

Fort William **13**, at the head of Loch Linnhe takes its name from the fort, now no more, established there for the military control of the Highlands. The older settlement of Inverlochy, scene of one of Montrose's victories, is near. The town, 'the capital of Lochaber', is overshadowed by mighty Ben Nevis (4,406 feet) **14**, seen across the head of the loch from Corpach. It is the highest mountain in the British Isles and climbers are often lost on its summit, where in winter arctic conditions are encountered.

Glenfinnan **15** at the northern end of Loch Shiel was the scene of the Gathering of the Clans for the Jacobite Rising of Bonnie Prince Charlie in 1745. The single column, with its figure of a kilted Highlander, commemorates those who sacrificed all in that ill-fated campaign. Further west, on the tip of Morar looking to Skye, we come to Mallaig **16**, a railway terminus and fishing port. From here there is communication by sea with Skye and with the Outer Isles, which lie across the stormy Minch. This is Jacobite country, for just as Glenfinnan saw the start of the '45, so Mallaig sheltered the fugitive Prince after Culloden.

From Fort William north-east to Inverness runs a geological fault known as the Great Glen. It contains three lochs, Ness, Oich and Lochy, which have been linked by the Caledonian Canal to give passage from the Moray Firth to the Firth of Lorne and the Atlantic. West of Loch Lochy lies Loch Arkaig **17** with Achnacarry, the home of Cameron of Lochiel, Chief of the clan of that name. Fort Augustus **18** is at the southern tip of Loch Ness (its name another reminder of troubled days of military occupation). Today war has yielded to piety and learning—the Benedictine Abbey and School may be seen on the left. Inverness-shire does not lack for grandeur, as in Glen Shiel **19**, with the Saddle ahead. Here we are in Kintail, one of the most spectacular districts of Wester Ross. It has been called 'the epitome of the West Highland scene' and the proportions of its mountains give a sense of majesty. To reach Kintail the visitor from the south strikes west from Invergarry on Loch Oich or from Invermoriston on Loch Ness. The roads unite at Cluanie Bridge amid the wildest desolation Scotland has to show. After rain the hillsides are at their most spectacular. White waterfalls appear in every cleft and modest streams are transformed into raging torrents.

17

19

20

21 22

The Five Sisters of Kintail **20** stand at the head of Loch Duich, the rhodo-
dendrons and azaleas reminding us that here on the western seaboard the
climate is mild, thanks to the influence of the Gulf Stream. The famous old
Mackenzie stronghold Eilean Donan Castle **21**, of which the Macraes were
hereditary constables, commands three lochs. It has been splendidly
restored in recent times. We are on the way to Skye, which may be reached
by Kyle of Lochalsh. But from afar off there are fine mountain views of the
Cuillin Hills **22**, seen here from Elgol on the opposite shore of Loch Scavaig.
A few miles to the north of Loch Alsh is lovely Loch Carron **23** with the
hills of the Applecross peninsula beyond. From many points on this coast
there are breath-catching views across the sea to the Cuillins and Blaven
in the Isle of Skye—air, sea and land in miraculous combination. Skye itself
may be reached from Kyle of Lochalsh. Glenelg or Mallaig. 'The Winged
Isle' is a paradise for climbers, after whom some of the peaks are named.

23

24

25

26   2

There can be no more dramatic mountain in all Scotland than Liathach **24**, as seen from across Loch Clair in Wester Ross. This peak also commands the upper end of the sea-Loch Torridon in a district scenically unspoilt. Loch Maree **25**, a long freshwater loch, is linked with Loch Ewe and the sea by the short River Ewe, a salmon stream. The notable semi-tropical gardens of Inverewe House may be visited here, another reminder of the remarkable climate at this northern latitude. The charming resort and fishing port of Ullapool **26** turns to advantage the shelter of Loch Broom. Further north again we pass the uncompromising Stac Polly **27** in a country beloved, as this picture tells us, by the stalker. Stac Pollaidh (to give it the Gaelic spelling) reaches a height of 2,009 feet. Like Liathach (3,456 feet) it is of red sandstone, but Liathach like its neighbour Ben Eighe has a cap of white quartzite. This region contains some of the most unspoilt scenery in Scotland.

28

This extraordinary platoon of mountains, drawn up in the Inverpolly and Glencanisp Forests **28**, reads from left to right, Suilven (2,399 feet) perhaps the best known of all the Sutherland mountains, Cul Mor (2,786 feet), Cul Peag (2,523 feet) and Stac Polly (2,009 feet). They are here seen from a point above the Bay of Stoer near Lochinver. Lochinver, with Suilven and Canisp **29** in the background, stands beyond Loch Inver, an estuary of the wide, island-studded Enard Bay. Here we have crossed from Wester Ross into the north-western county of Scotland, Sutherland of the tortured mountains, peat mosses and stony moors with many a lovely strath once peopled by crofting folk until sheep and the evictions brought their tenure to an abrupt end. Canada and New Zealand offered a home for the dis-possessed people in one of the saddest episodes of Scottish history—the reason why many of their Prime Ministers bear Scots names.

30

31 **3**

32

A string of lochs keeps company with the road from Lairg to Laxford Bridge in Sutherland and of these Loch Merkland **30** is one. The boat drawn up on the strand reminds us that they are a paradise of fly fishermen. On the northern coast of Sutherland (so named because it was 'South-land' to the Vikings) the Kyle of Tongue **31** opens on the sea, watched over by magnificent Ben Loyal (2,504 feet). Turning south from this northernmost point of the Scottish mainland, we return to Ross and Cromarty, and find gentle Loch Luichart **32**, crescent-shaped and birch-fringed, to the south of the road that leads west from Inverness through Strath Bran. Journeying south and east from Inverness we come to the broad and impetuous River Spey **33**, here shown in its severe upper reaches near Garva. The Spey, rising in the Corrieyairack Forest, drops 1,143 feet to the sea in its course of 107 miles. Many fishermen hold this to be the finest salmon river.

The Eastern Highlands have their glories as well as the West, and of these the chief is the Cairngorm Range. Though Ben Macdhui had to yield its claim to be the highest mountain in Scotland to Ben Nevis, the group with its numerous lofty peaks, savage passes and lonely lochans is as a whole unsurpassed as territory for the hill-walker. Looking across the Forest of Rothiemurchus on Speyside we see snow-capped Cairn Gorm itself **34**, not the highest of the range at 4,084 feet, and Corrie Raibeirt. The River Dee rises among these hills, then flows east to the sea at Aberdeen. If we strike south from Braemar at the head of the valley, we pass the Spittal of Glenshee **35**, in its isolation at the foot of Ben Gulabin. This has since the Second World War become an important ski-ing centre. Still further south again, in Perthshire, the country assumes a richer and more welcoming appearance, thanks perhaps to the luxuriance of the trees which clothe hillside and river bank. The wooded valley of the River Tummel near Pitlochry **36** shows Perthshire scenery at its best. At Pitlochry itself the Festival Theatre entertains its patrons every year from April to October, with a different play on every night of the week.

34

36

37

Even in Perthshire, which lies so close to the centre of Scotland, there are
tracts of great solitude, and Loch Rannoch **37** with the Moor of Rannoch to
the west, is at the heart of one of these. Flanked by high hills, among them
Schiehallion, it mirrors the moods of the ever-changing sky. All the Perthshire lochs are long and narrow. Loch Tay **38** stretches for nearly fifteen
miles from Killin at its head to Kenmore, from which point the River Tay,
the longest in Scotland, issues on a course which passes the town of Perth
and ends in the Firth of Tay, beside Dundee. Both the loch and the river
are noted for the quality of the salmon fishing, and indeed all the Highlands appeal to the sportsmen as much as to the lover of scenery.

38